The Coming Glory

The Coming Glory

HOPE NOW FOR LIFE AFTER DEATH

Paul W. Swets

CrossLink Publishing
RAPID CITY, SD

Swets/CrossLink Publishing
1601 Mt Rushmore Rd, Ste 3288
Rapid City, SD 57701
www.crosslinkpublishing.com

Ordering Information:
Special discounts are available on quantity purchases by corporations, associations, and others. For details, contact the "Special Sales Department" at the address above.

The Coming Glory/Paul Swets. —1st ed.
ISBN 978-1-63357-163-1
Library of Congress Control Number: 2018958687
First edition: 10 9 8 7 6 5 4 3 2 1

Reader Comments

In *The Coming Glory*, Paul Swets gives an elegant and yet direct account of Christian hope for the dying. Utilizing his wisdom from years of pastoral work, Swets offers a compelling taste of Christian hope that is accessible to a very broad audience.

—**Dr. J. Todd Billings**
Author of *Rejoicing in Lament: Wrestling with Incurable Cancer and Life in Christ*

GLORIOUS!! I have just finished reading *The Coming Glory* and I have tears in my eyes, thinking of the people who will be comforted and encouraged through the last stage of their earthly journey, and their loved ones too. So much to love about this book—it is saturated in Scripture, Paul's pastor's heart shines through every word, it is theologically rich, and the whole gospel is here. The way the author weaves in the great hymns and confessions of the faith is beautiful.

—Rev. Dr. Suzanne McDonald
Professor of Historical and Systematic Theology

When I was a pastor, I would have been delighted to have had these concise, well-crafted treatments of key eschatological themes. I would have valued especially a book like this to put in the hands of laypeople facing death, along with their caring families. We meet a warm pastoral tone throughout the book. Readers will sense that they are hearing from a man with long experience and a caring heart.

—Rev. Dr. William C. Brownson
President Emeritus, Words of Hope

So encouraging! I couldn't put it down. *The Coming Glory* would be a wonderful book for a small group book study. I like the large print. I was comforted by the appropriately placed Scripture and hymns. Paul has offered answers to seekers and those looking toward eternity.

—Marty Greendonner
Retired Teacher

The abundance of Scripture is the most valuable part of *The Coming Glory*. By bringing together quotes from throughout the New Testament, this book is able to give a fuller sense of the Bible's perspective on some big questions and answers. The use of many short quotes followed by commentary was effective at bringing out the meaning.

—Rev. Nicholas Monco, OP
Diocese of Grand Rapids

The Coming Glory beautifully presents the end of our earthly lives in terms of a natural departure, leaving one place to go to another. Through an instructive lineup of Bible verses, Paul Swets shows how to find comfort for the journey and how you can know for certain that the astounding good news of heaven is for you!

—**Carla Sinnema**
Teacher

Tremendously inspiring! *The Coming Glory* is full of words that speak to the mind, heart, and soul with confidence and assurance as we face death. It would be an immensely helpful tool for ministers to give to parishioners facing life-and-death situations.

—**Rev. Dr. John W. Tien**
Retired Pastor

Having lost my spouse, I turned to sources of comfort and assurance. Grief and uncertainty occupied my thoughts. I found answers in *The Coming Glory*. Death brings loss and is certain. But this book offers life and hope that we survivors all need for continuing our lives on earth. I thank God that Paul Swets wrote this book. I recommend it to everyone, especially those who find themselves perplexed by the same questions I faced.

—**Dr. Rodger Rice**
Emeritus Professor of Sociology,
Calvin College

The Coming Glory feeds its readers actual bread, rather than merely the stone of human opinion. The author's own constant reliance on Scripture gives readers like me confidence that they can depend on the promises and hope described in this book. Swets points readers to the gospel and to the person at the heart of it—Jesus. He shows why the gospel is the natural response to

many of the fears and challenges people may have about departing this life.
—**Dr. Han-luen Kantzer Komline**
*Assistant Professor of Church History
and Theology*

Dedication

The Coming Glory is dedicated to individuals and families who suffer the grief of impending death and want true hope.

*Why are you cast down, O my soul,
and why are you in turmoil within me?
Hope in God; for I shall again praise
him, my salvation and my God.*

PSALM 42:5–6

*I consider that the sufferings of
this present time are not worth
comparing with the glory
that is to be revealed to us.*

ROMANS 8:18

Contents

Foreword

*T*he *Coming Glory* is a gentle word for a difficult time.

Paul offers an honest, truthful, and hopeful journey for any facing the reality of death. It will honor your journey. It will awaken you to a future hard to imagine. It will prayerfully hold your hand as you walk through the valley.

Frankly, I couldn't stop reading *The Coming Glory*. I was moved by the truth, I was moved by Paul's honesty, I was moved by his courage. I was moved to tears by this last paragraph: "The time for my departure is getting closer day by day. Although I deeply love this life,

I can hardly wait for the coming glory."
—Rev. Dr. Jon Brown
Lead Pastor, Pillar Church

A Note to the Reader

Death is not the end of our story. Glory is coming!

Life would be senseless, absurd, and tragic if death were the final chapter of our story. Of course, it is no good to concoct an imagined future in order to feel better. We need truth—truth that draws us closer to the Author of our faith and prepares us for the coming glory.

Professor J. Todd Billings, who is wrestling with incurable cancer, writes, "For true hope in the face of death, we have nowhere else to go besides the Word of God, which finds its fulfillment in Jesus Christ."[1]

The Coming Glory will help you catch a glimpse of what the Word of

God teaches about life after death and what is ahead for you. Scripture reveals that the coming glory is the presence and power of God manifested in Christ and all His redeeming work. Our appropriate response is wonder, awe, and worship.

Mystery is abundant. The Bible doesn't tell us everything. The apostle Paul acknowledges that there is so much more ahead than we can know now. As he considers the fact of the resurrection of Jesus Christ and the hope this gives to you and me, he exclaims:

> *No eye has seen, nor ear heard,*
> *nor the heart of man imagined,*
> *what God has prepared*
> *for those who love him.*
>
> 1 CORINTHIANS 2:9–10

Like many Christians, you might be confused about the mystery of what is ahead. Yet what the Bible does reveal is a true future reality glorious beyond compare.

Death is a present reality that stirs fearful emotions now. You likely have a bundle of feelings that must not be stifled—shock, depression, panic, guilt, anger, hope.

Please share your story and questions with a friend or a pastor—someone who will hear you out and listen to your soul. Most importantly, pour out your anguish to the Wonderful Counselor, who loves you and knows you better than you know yourself.

As a minister of pastoral care, I have had the privilege of hearing the stories of hundreds of individuals and families in the midst of life-and-death crises. You might think of this little book as a friend that comes alongside you and gives you hope.

Notes found at the back of the book provide information on source materials and biblical content not directly included in the text. Also, there are chapter summaries that give brief answers to each chapter question, and a recommended reading list.

Dear friend, God's gospel can move us from anxious despair into calm assurance and true hope. My prayer is that the Holy Spirit will excite our minds and comfort our hearts with the plain (but mysterious) and simple (but profound) truth of the gospel.

—Paul W. Swets
Holland, Michigan

*Brothers and sisters, we do not
want you to be uninformed about
those who sleep in death,
so that you do not grieve
like the rest of mankind,
who have no hope.*

1 THESSALONIANS 4:13 NIV

CHAPTER 1

How Can I Prepare for My Departure?

The time of my departure has come.
The Apostle Paul
2 TIMOTHY 4:6

Departure is a gentle way of saying the apostle Paul knew he was about to die.

You or a family member may be at this same point of "departure." It is hard to accept this reality. We don't want to depart from all we know. We don't want to leave our loved ones. We fear suffering—our own and that of our loved ones. We don't know what's on "the other side." We grieve deeply. Our sorrow, fear, and confusion are understandable.

In the midst of his suffering and grief, the psalmist pleaded with the Lord in this prayer of lament:

> *Be merciful to me, Lord,*
> *for I am in distress; my*
> *eyes grow weak with sorrow, my soul*
> *and body with grief.*
> *My life is consumed by anguish*
> *and my years by groaning;*
> *my strength fails*
> *because of my affliction,*
> *and my bones grow weak.*
> PSALM 31:9–10 NIV

Thankfully, God hears our cries of lament, our passionate expressions of grief, even our anger.

The Lord has heard my plea;
the Lord accepts my prayer.
PSALM 6:9

The Lord hears us! And He will answer according to what is best for us—but not always the way we want Him to answer. God is God, and we are not.

Mike prayed for relief, but he was dying. He knew it; his family knew it. He was firm in his faith. The family thought he was well prepared for death, but near the time for his departure, he said, "I'm confused." For the first time, he was face-to-face with an enormous new reality—his impending death. His uncertainty made him very uncomfortable.

Mike is like many facing their last days. I have had the privilege of coming alongside hundreds of them with their families—waiting, listening, comforting. I remember the intense emotions in the midst of grief: fear and confusion, yet sometimes magnificent peace and calm.

How do you or I prepare for death? After a heart attack, a quintuple-bypass surgery, a TAVR surgery, and an ongoing Inclusion Body Myositis condition, I ponder this sobering question. It motivates me to prepare for my own departure.

Departure is the word Paul chooses—not *dissolution*, not *destruction*, not *annihilation*. *Departure* suggests leaving one place in order to go to another place, like a ship departing from one port to go to another port. Some have likened the death of a believer to leaving earth's shore, ideally with supportive family and friends gathered around, and arriving at heaven's shore to the cheers of the waiting heavenly host.

You or your loved one might be facing a departure now. Questions abound, not only about procedural details, but also about *what happens to you after you leave earth's shore*. What you have believed all your life might not be clear or comforting. Perhaps you, like most of us, have not thought about the spiritual implications of death for yourself or your family members...until now. Now is the best time to make sense of your condition. You can choose now to learn and believe the hope the Scripture teaches.

Learn from the apostle Paul. Paul knew he would die soon. He accepted it. In fact, he even looked forward to it. Why? He was convinced that:

For me to live is Christ,
and to die is gain.
PHILIPPIANS 1:21

In his letter to Timothy, Paul mentioned three actions that had prepared him to depart in peace:

I have fought the good fight,
I have finished the race,
I have kept the faith.

2 TIMOTHY 4:7

You and I might think we cannot say this with the confidence of Paul. After all, he was an apostle. But even Paul admitted times of great failure:

I do not understand my
own actions. For I do not
do what I want, but I do
the very thing I hate.

ROMANS 7:15

Even though Paul regularly failed to live up to all his intentions, he was able to affirm three major facts about his life.

"I have fought the good fight."

Paul drew this image from his love of sports. In several other places, he used metaphors from the Olympic games: fighting, running, training, and winning.

Notice, Paul wrote, "I have fought the good *fight*..." Life is a battleground. Death is an enemy. Paul understands our struggle for faith, especially critical when death looms and suffering, doubt, or temptation overwhelm. To Timothy and to every believer, Paul encouraged the fight against unbelief:

> *Fight the good fight of the faith. Take hold of the eternal life to which you were called....*
>
> 1 TIMOTHY 6:12

If you have been hurt in this fight, or if you feel you have already lost the battle for faith, do not despair. Victory is still possible. Even in the midst of doubt, call upon Jesus for help.

Remember the father who came to Jesus and said this:

I believe; help my unbelief.
MARK 9:24

When you ask Jesus to help you believe in Him, Jesus will, indeed, help you. Then the amazing truth of the gospel will apply to you:

Death is swallowed up in victory.
1 CORINTHIANS 15:54

Paul was saying that your death is not the end of the story. Christ's resurrection guarantees your victory. It's like the D-Day of World War II. Because the decisive battle had already been won, victory was assured. Christ's resurrection is the decisive victory over death, and it's a preview of the coming glory.

The strife is o'er, the battle done;
The victory of life is won;
The song of triumph has begun.
Alleluia![1]

"I have finished the race."

Think about the times when you worked long and hard on a project and then experienced the joy of finishing it. Finish-line joy related to completing one's life task was brought home to me in a shocking way. My family had gathered around my father's hospital bed as he was getting ready for his departure. Suddenly, with unusual strength, he sat up in bed, clapped his hands, and with a look of triumph said, "I'm dying!"

Did my father somehow hear "the distant triumph song"?

And when the strife is fierce,
the warfare long, steals on
the ear the distant triumph song,
and hearts are brave again,
and arms are strong.
Alleluia, alleluia![2]

"I have kept the faith."

What does it mean to *keep* the faith? It means to commit to, to persevere, to maintain faith in Jesus even when the fight is hard and the failures are many. It means to keep on believing in Jesus in spite of our botches.

For God so loved the world
that he gave his only Son, that
whoever believes in him should
not perish but have eternal life.

JOHN 3:16

*If you confess with your mouth
that Jesus is Lord and believe in
your heart that God raised him
from the dead, you will be saved.*

ROMANS 10:9

Does the Bible imply that all we need to do is just say the words and all will be well? No! What we confess with our mouth needs to come from the heart, the very core of our being. When our confession of faith is authentic, we will aim to believe and act in a way that fits a follower of Christ.

*And by this we know
that we have come to know [Jesus],
if we keep his commandments.*

1 JOHN 2:3

Jesus summarized the commandments of God:

*You shall love the Lord your
God with all your heart and
with all your soul and with all
your mind. This is the great
and first commandment. And
a second is like it: You shall
love your neighbor as yourself.*

MATTHEW 22:37–39

None of us has ever believed God
or kept His commandments perfectly.
But we can take heart, because Jesus
paid the penalty for our sin through
His death on the cross and He offers
forgiveness to all who trust in Him.

*God demonstrates his own love
for us in this: While we were
still sinners, Christ died for us.*

ROMANS 5:8 NIV

*There is therefore now no
condemnation for those*

who are in Christ Jesus.
ROMANS 8:1

It's never too late to ask Jesus to help you trust in Him, to declare with your heart and your mind as the early Christians did: "Jesus is my Lord!" This heartfelt affirmation enables you to experience the refreshment of God's complete forgiveness of your sin.

Repent, then, and turn to God,
so that your sins may be wiped out,
that times of refreshing
may come from the Lord....
ACTS 3:19 NIV

Repentance of sin and faith in Christ send peace into your soul.

****

Summary

You can prepare for your departure by affirming your belief in Jesus Christ, who loves you and gives you eternal life.

Prayer

God, it's hard to get through my head that while I am yet a sinner, You still love me and want to save me.

I confess that I have not followed Your commandments perfectly. I am sorry.

Please forgive my sins.

Thank You for Your love, shown to me in Jesus. Please give me faith that Christ is the One who will save me, just as I am, and give me hope now for life after death. Amen.

Reflection

1. What feelings or thoughts do you have about your departure or that of a loved one?
2. How do you relate to the apostle Paul's statement about his preparation for departure: "*I have fought the good fight, I have finished the race, I have kept the faith*"?
3. How prepared are you for your departure?
4. What comfort in this chapter will you focus on?

Into your hand
I commit my spirit;
you have redeemed me,
O LORD, faithful God....
I trust in you, O Lord;
I say, "You are my God."
My times are in your hand.

PSALM 31:5, 15

CHAPTER 2

What Happens Right after Death?

*We would rather be away from the body
and at home with the Lord.*

2 CORINTHIANS 5:8

Home! What does "home" mean to you? At best, the idea of our earthly home includes:

- Family that brings out the best in each other.
- Feeling safe in an atmosphere of love.

- The place where we don't have to hide who we are.

After death, we have a home that will surpass the best this life can offer, because we will be "at home with the Lord."

When the apostle Paul said that he would rather be *"away from the body and at home with the Lord,"* he was referring to heaven, or paradise, the intermediate state between a Christian's death and the resurrection of the body. When we die, our physical bodies will be left behind here on earth, but our souls (the unique personalities that make us different from every other person) will go immediately into the presence of Christ. Jesus said to the thief on the cross:

*Truly I tell you, today you
will be with me in paradise.*
LUKE 23:43 NIV

"Paradise" refers to a state of restful happiness in the presence of the Lord Jesus. Theologian N.T. Wright explains the meaning of paradise: "This state is not, clearly, the final destiny for which the Christian dead are bound, which is the bodily resurrection. But it is a state in which the dead are held firmly within the conscious love of God and the conscious presence of Jesus Christ while they await that day."[1]

The Bible does not tell us a great deal about this intermediate state. Lack of detail is part of the grand mystery of God. But the Bible does reveal what happens when believers die: They enter a state of being "at home with the Lord"—*a joyful awareness of being with Jesus*—which Paul exclaims is "far better."

"Far better?" You and I might find it hard to agree that we would rather be "away from the body." Most of us have a built-in, God-given desire to live as long as we can, unless suffering or despair overwhelm us in the present.

Yet Paul asserts it is *far better* for us to be away from the body, because our souls will be "at home with the Lord." That means that departure from the body at death is not a journey into nothingness or unconsciousness or sleep. Rather, it is a journey of the believer's soul into the very presence of Christ. The soul will be *with Christ*. We will be with the One who gave His very life to rescue us *from* a hellish state *for* triumphant glory!

Compared to the coming glory, any suffering we go through now will fade into insignificance.

For I consider that the sufferings
of this present time are not

worth comparing with the glory
that is to be revealed to us.
ROMANS 8:18

A mother submits to the pains of labor because of the anticipated joy of holding her newborn. When God's glory is fully revealed, every believer in Christ will revel in the joy of God's promises fulfilled.

Not all of God's promises are completely fulfilled at death. We must still await the promise of the resurrection of our bodies. But immediately after we die, our souls will be at home with the Lord, and that will be glory unveiled for every believer.

Going home, going home,
I'm just going home.
Quiet-like, slip away—
I'll be going home.

It's not far, just close by;
Jesus is the Door;
Work all done, laid aside,
Fear and grief no more.
Friends are there,
waiting now.
He is waiting, too.
See His smile! See His hand!
He will lead me through.[2]

******

Summary

Right after death, the soul (the true identity) of the believer is "at home with the Lord," and that is better than we can ever imagine.

Prayer

Precious Lord, take my hand,
lead me on, help me stand;
I am tired, I am weak,

I am worn;
through the storm,
through the night,
lead me on to the light;
take my hand, precious Lord,
lead me home.[3]

Reflection

1. What does the idea of "home" mean to you?
2. What images come to mind in being "at home with the Lord"?
3. From what current suffering do you long to be freed?
4. On what comfort in this chapter will you choose to focus?

We know that if the tent that is our earthly home is destroyed, we have a building from God, a house not made with hands, eternal in the heavens.

2 CORINTHIANS 5:1

CHAPTER 3

How Can I Get Ready for the Return of Christ?

You also must be ready,
for the Son of Man is coming
at an hour you do not expect.

MATTHEW 24:44

The history of our world is moving toward a tremendous climax—*the return of Christ to this earth!*

Christ's return is a key teaching of the New Testament:

*I will come again and will
take you to myself, that
where I am you may be also.*
JOHN 14:3

*This Jesus, who was taken
up from you into heaven,
will come in the same way
as you saw him go into heaven.*
ACTS 1:11

Mindful of our limited understanding of the coming glory that will take place when Jesus appears, consider the following amazing events that Scripture indicates will occur:

- Dead bodies will be resurrected.[1]
- The world as we know it will end and be transformed into a new creation.[2]
- Christ will reign as Lord.[3]
- The final judgment will occur.[4]
- Unbelievers will be judged in their sins.[5]

- Believers will be welcomed in their faith.[6]
- Believers will experience heaven on the new earth.[7]

At one time scientists thought the earth was eternal, that it had always existed. Since that time, however, scientists have discovered facts similar to what the Bible teaches: There was a beginning,[8] and there will be an end.[9] Scripture teaches that the end of history, as we know it now, will happen when Christ returns to usher in the "new heavens and new earth."[10] (See Chapter 6.)

If the return of Christ to earth staggers your imagination, good! You're on the right track. Nothing in our personal experience will compare to Christ's return.

Like the miracle of the "Incarnation"—*God taking on human flesh in Jesus Christ*—Christ's return will be a miracle of gigantic proportion.

If it were not for the almighty power of God, who *created the universe*, the return of Christ would seem more like a wish than a future reality.

Scripture declares that we all will experience this future event.

Every eye will see him.
REVELATION 1:7

The return of Christ is such a significant development in God's redemptive plan that it's important to think about it now, even in the midst of our distress.

Christ's return motivates us to *prepare* now for His coming, to experience the joyful *hope* that His return provides, and to *wait* with courage and perseverance for the fulfillment of all of God's promises in Christ.

Prepare

Jesus taught about being ready for His return using four parables or stories. Each illustrates this theme:

> *Therefore you also must be ready,*
> *for the Son of Man is coming*
> *at an hour you do not expect.*
> MATTHEW 24:44

One of the stories is about ten virgins anticipating a wedding.[11] Five wise virgins had adequate oil for their lamps and were welcomed into the wedding feast. Five virgins were foolish because they had not made adequate preparation. They were not allowed into the wedding feast. The point of the story is to plan ahead and be ready for the coming of the Bridegroom, i.e., the return of Christ.

You might be like the wise virgins, who were prepared. You have prepared yourself by receiving Christ into your heart by faith. Or you might be like the foolish virgins, who were not ready, who thought they would have plenty of time later to prepare. Christ taught that because we do not know when the Son of Man (Jesus) will come, we should prepare now by believing in Christ so that our lives will be in order now, prepared for eternity.

*I tell you, now is the
time of God's favor,
now is the day of salvation.*
2 CORINTHIANS 6:2 NIV

Hope

When you receive Christ's offer of salvation through faith in Him, you can have hope—a rock-solid confidence that Jesus will return and that He has prepared a place for you.

Let not your hearts be troubled.
Believe in God; believe also in me.
In my Father's house are
many rooms. If it were not so,
would I have told you that
I go to prepare a place for you?
And if I go and prepare a place
for you, I will come again and
will take you to myself, that
where I am you may be also.
JOHN 14:1–3

Oh, what comfort! Christ promises a place for believers to dwell, a place prepared by Christ Himself! Christ's promise provides inner peace now, even in the midst of our turmoil. We tend to be quickly troubled by many things—real, serious, immediate things—that can rob us of deep peace. Even so, Jesus made it clear that peace is available to us in spite of our troubles.

I have said these things to you,
that in me you may have peace.
In the world you will have tribulation.
But take heart;
I have overcome the world.

JOHN 16:33

Peace is based on the certain hope we have in Christ now—hope because Christ has promised that those who believe in Him will be saved.

Let us hold fast the confession
of our hope without wavering,
for he who promised is faithful.

HEBREWS 10:23

At the return of Christ, we will also experience the resurrection of the body (discussed in the next chapter). This hope motivates us to affirm the following:

Christ has died.
Christ is risen.
Christ will come again.[12]

This is our hope now for eternity.

When he shall come
with trumpet sound,
O may I then
in him be found,
dressed in his
righteousness alone,
faultless to stand
before the throne.
On Christ, the solid rock,
I stand; All other ground
is sinking sand.[13]

Wait

The New Testament stresses the certainty of Christ's return. For example, the last book of the Bible concludes with this promise of Jesus:

Surely I am coming soon.
REVELATION 22:20

"Soon"? Perhaps you are asking, "Why, then, must we wait? Why is the return of Christ so long in coming?" You and I are not alone in asking, "Why the wait?" Even shortly after the resurrection of Christ, the apostle Peter records that some were asking this very question:

> *Where is this "coming" he*
> *promised? Ever since our*
> *ancestors died, everything*
> *goes on as it has since*
> *the beginning of creation.*
> 2 PETER 3:4 NIV

Peter explains God's purpose for the delay:

> *Do not overlook this one fact,*
> *beloved, that with the Lord*

one day is as a thousand years,
and a thousand years as one day.
The Lord is not slow to
fulfill his promise as some
count slowness, but is patient
toward you, not wishing that
any should perish, but that
all should reach repentance.

2 PETER 3:8–9

Did you get that? The reason for the wait is God's mercy and love for you and all of the people in the world. He wants us all to repent and receive His gracious call to believe in Jesus.

Christ, having been offered
once to bear the sins of many,
will appear a second time, not
to deal with sin but to save those
who are eagerly waiting for him.

HEBREWS 9:28

Think of it! Salvation's result is complete liberation from sin and an unhindered fellowship with Christ when He returns. Is the wait worth it?

Wendell Kimbrough relates in song the Christian's emotions while waiting and hoping:

Now the days and hours and moments
of suffering seem so long,
and the toilsome wait and wondering
threaten silence to our song.
Now our pain is real and pressing
where our faith is thin and weak,
but our hope is set on Jesus
and we cling to him, our strength.[14]

****

Summary

When we set our hope on Jesus, who is our strength and who comforts us in our weakness, we will be ready for the return of Christ.

Prayer

Almighty God—Father, Son, and Holy Spirit—I praise You that in Your great mercy, You give all believers new birth into a living hope through the resurrection of Jesus Christ from the dead. I rejoice in the hope of the future return of Christ and an inheritance that can never perish, spoil, or fade.

Please help me in my suffering and grief. May my faith prove genuine and result in praise, glory, and honor now and when Jesus Christ comes again. Come, Lord Jesus. Amen.

—A prayer based on 1 PETER 1:3–9

Reflection

1. As you get ready for the return of Christ, what do you find most challenging?
2. On what comfort in this chapter will you choose to focus?

Be still before the Lord and wait patiently for him....

PSALM 37:7

CHAPTER 4

What Will Our Bodily Resurrection Be Like?

Behold! I tell you a mystery. We shall not all sleep, but we shall all be changed, in a moment, in the twinkling of an eye, at the last trumpet. For the trumpet will sound, and the dead will be raised imperishable, and we shall be changed.

1 CORINTHIANS 15:51–52

66 "The dead will be raised!" "We shall be changed!" At death, we shall rest in peace (at home with the Lord), but

at the return of Christ, *we shall rise in glory*. Mystery, indeed!

Scripture provides only faint indications of what the resurrection of our bodies will be like. And that may be all our finite minds can handle for the time being.

In this chapter, we look at the glimpses we do have in Scripture about what the future holds for us—a coming glory beyond compare.

We know that when he [Jesus]
appears we shall be like him,
because we shall see him as he is.
1 JOHN 3:2

The resurrection of Christ assures us of our own bodily resurrection. We shall be like Him!

Our Historical Foundation

Historical fact lays the groundwork for our hope. We are not talking about wish fulfillment or mystic vision or conjecture. God's power raised Jesus Christ—body and soul—from the dead. This is the historical basis for the hope of our own bodily resurrection.

Even before the event of the resurrection, Jesus promised His disciples that He would be raised from the dead:

From that time Jesus began to show his disciples that he must go to Jerusalem and suffer many things... and be killed, and on the third day be raised.
MATTHEW 16:21

Jesus does not merely say that He will be raised (which is true), but His statement is much stronger. To Martha at the death of Lazarus, Jesus declared:

I am the resurrection and the life.
Whoever believes in me,
though he die, yet shall he live.

JOHN 11:25

Shortly after this conversation with Martha, Jesus died on the cross to pay the penalty for our sin. He was buried, and then God raised Him to life—a resurrection event that changed history and undergirds the Christian faith. Matthew records what happened:

On the first day of the week,
at early dawn, they went to
the tomb, taking the spices
they had prepared. And they
found the stone rolled away
from the tomb, but when they
went in they did not find the
body of the Lord Jesus. While
they were perplexed about this,
behold, two men stood by
them in dazzling apparel.

*And as they were frightened
and bowed their faces to the
ground, the men said to them,
"Why do you seek the living
among the dead? He is not here,
but has risen. Remember how
he told you, while he was still
in Galilee, that the Son of Man
must be delivered into the
hands of sinful men and be
crucified and on the third day rise."*

LUKE 24:1–7

The apostle Paul recounts the historical appearances of Christ after His resurrection:

*For I delivered to you as of
first importance what I also
received: that Christ died for
our sins in accordance with
the Scriptures, that he was
buried, that he was raised on
the third day...and that he*

appeared to Cephas, then to the twelve. Then he appeared to more than five hundred brothers at one time.... Then he appeared to James, then to all the apostles. Last of all, as to one untimely born, he appeared also to me.

1 CORINTHIANS 15:3–8

It is because of the historical fact of the resurrection of Christ that we have hope for our own resurrection. Death is not the end of our story, but our entry into eternal life. Referring to this hope, the apostle Peter praises God for Jesus' resurrection and what it means for us:

Blessed be the God and Father of our Lord Jesus Christ! According to his great mercy, he has caused us to be born again to a living hope through the resurrection of Jesus Christ from the dead....

1 PETER 1:3

Peter mentions "living hope" because Jesus' resurrection guarantees to us now that our bodies will be resurrected. Especially now, in the midst of suffering, our individual resurrection gives us hope. We can view our future as dynamic, exciting, awe-inspiring.

A Helpful Analogy

It would be foolish to think we can comprehend everything about our resurrected body. Yet the apostle Paul helps us understand what we can know by comparing our earthly bodies to a seed:

> *What you sow does not come to life unless it dies. And what you sow is not the body that is to be, but a bare kernel, perhaps of wheat or of some other grain. But God gives it a body as he has chosen, and to each kind of*

*seed its own body. For not all flesh
is the same, but there is one kind for
humans, another for animals,
another for birds, and another for
fish. There are heavenly bodies and
earthly bodies, but the glory of
the heavenly is of one kind, and the
glory of the earthly is of another.*

1 CORINTHIANS 15:36–40

Paul's analogy suggests there will be a *continuity* between our present selves and our resurrected selves—it's the same "seed." But there will be also a vast *difference*—now our bodies are a "bare kernel" compared to the fully developed resurrected body.

A Clear Comparison

Paul expands the description of our resurrected bodies by contrasting it with our earthly bodies.

1. Perishable versus Imperishable

What is sown is perishable;
what is raised is imperishable.
1 CORINTHIANS 15:42

Our present bodies are perishable; the seeds of death and disease are in them so that it's only a matter of time before they die. But we shall be raised imperishable. No more death, no more mourning, no more crying, no more pain.[1]

2. Dishonor versus Glory

It is sown in dishonor;
it is raised in glory.
1 CORINTHIANS 15:43

Our bodies now are not perfect. We all have some defects that afflict the body, including sin. But our resurrected bodies will be glorious—not just on the outside, but they will also have a glory from inside the transformed person. PHILIPPIANS 3:21 says that Christ will transform our lowly bodies to be like His glorious body—a real physical body that reflects the glory of God.

Can you imagine what your body will be like minus all imperfections? No sin. No guilt. No mobility or other physical issues. Theologian Anthony Hoekema says, "We shall not really know what this glory is like until we ourselves shall see it and experience it."[2]

3. Weakness versus Power

It is sown in weakness;
it is raised in power.
1 CORINTHIANS 15:43

If you are like me, you get tired. You can't accomplish all you would like to do. You are always conscious of your limitations. As death approaches—either gradually, or instantly as in an accident or heart attack—we become totally weak, helpless. But at the time of the resurrection, this weak body will be raised in power. Can you imagine what your body "raised in power" will be like?

4. Natural versus Spiritual

It is sown a natural body;
it is raised a spiritual body.
1 CORINTHIANS 15:44

A *spiritual body* is not the opposite of a *physical body*. Christ's resurrected body was definitely a physical one— He could be touched (JOHN 20:17, 27); He could eat food (LUKE 24:38–43). But Christ's resurrected body was more than just physical; it was also spiritual, a transformed physicality. *Our resurrected bodies will be more than physical, but not less than physical.* In other words, our resurrected bodies will be like Christ's resurrected body.

> *Our citizenship is in heaven,*
> *and from it we await a Savior,*
> *the Lord Jesus Christ, who will*
> *transform our lowly body to be*
> *like his glorious body, by the*
> *power that enables him even to*
> *subject all things to himself.*
> PHILIPPIANS 3:20–21

Anthony Hoekema explains the viewpoint of Scripture on this point: "Matter is not evil; it is part of God's good creation. Therefore the goal of God's redemption is the resurrection of the physical body, and the creation of a new earth on which his redeemed people can live and serve God forever with glorified bodies."[3]

In the midst of suffering, Paul assures us of God's plan for us in our future:

> *He who raised Christ Jesus from the dead will also give life to your mortal bodies.*
>
> ROMANS 8:11

> *We ourselves...wait eagerly for... the redemption of our bodies.*
>
> ROMANS 8:23

What do these verses mean for you and me? Scripture teaches us that there will be a change from our natural, weak, perishable bodies to transformed, resurrected bodies. When that happens, we will experience on the new earth the full blessings that God provides.

Will we recognize family and friends in their resurrection bodies? That is our heart-warming hope. The disciples recognized Jesus in His resurrected body:

Although the Bible tells us very little about the exact nature of the resurrected body, we do know that when our resurrected bodies are like Christ's glorious body (PHILIPPIANS 3:20–21), they will not be subject to decay or death. At the return of Christ, our bodies will be more wonderful than our grandest hopes.

****

Summary

The Bible describes our resurrected bodies as imperishable, glorious, powerful, spiritual bodies. This gives us hope now, knowing that God will give us the final victory over every consequence of sin.

Prayer

O God, our help in the past and our hope for the future, open our eyes to Your truth so that we may know You better, see our future more clearly, and face even suffering and death now with calm assurance, knowing that our bodies will be resurrected through Jesus Christ, our risen Lord. Amen.

Reflection

1. What is the historical foundation for understanding the resurrection of the body?
2. What impresses you the most about the Bible's description of the resurrected body?
3. On what comfort in this chapter will you choose to focus?

I was brutish and ignorant;
I was like a beast toward you.
Nevertheless, I am continually
with you; you hold my right hand. You
guide me with your counsel,
and afterward you will
receive me to glory.

PSALM 73:22–24

CHAPTER 5

How Can I Face God's Judgment?

When justice is done, it is a joy to the righteous but terror to evildoers.

PROVERBS 21:15

B ecause none of us has lived a perfect life, we may wonder how we will survive the judgment of God. Is God's judgment a source of joy or terror for us?

In this chapter, we look at Scripture passages that remind us of who God is.

We focus on His gracious offer to escape the judgment our sin deserves.

Remember Who God Is

Even now, when the course of our lives does not go according to our plans, sometimes we wonder whether God is judging us.

Professor Todd Billings is considered by all who know him to be a very good person, but at the age of thirty-nine and with a wife and young children, he learned he has incurable cancer. It's normal for him to ask, "Why?"

Perhaps you ask, "Why?" *Why must I or my loved ones suffer? Why do bad things happen to good people? Are these events evidence of God's judgment against us?* Todd's condition motivated a vigorous search in Scripture for answers. He found guidance in the book of Job.

Job also was considered a good man, but some terrible things happened to his family and to him physically. Yet in the midst of intense suffering, Job gave clear testimony of his confidence in the future justice of God:

> I know that my Redeemer lives,
> and at the last he will stand upon
> the earth. And after my skin has
> been thus destroyed, yet in my
> flesh I shall see God, whom I
> shall see for myself....
> My heart faints within me!
>
> JOB 19:25–27

Even with Job's overwhelming confidence that he would "see God" after death, Job *lamented* his present condition. He was in anguish because his suffering did not seem to be just. Something was not right. The opinions of his friends were not much help, either. He presented his case to God.

The Creator of the universe counseled Job to be mentally tough and to reflect on the vast difference between his limited understanding and the infinite wisdom of God:

> *Who is this that darkens counsel*
> *by words without knowledge?...*
> *Where were you when I laid the*
> *foundation of the earth? Tell me,*
> *if you have understanding.*
>
> JOB 38:2, 4

Todd Billings comments, "In the end, after presenting his case to God that the Almighty has been unjust, Job hears God's response and is brought to the point of recanting his case. But Job does not confess *lament* as a sin against God, for it is not. Rather he comes to recognize the limits of human wisdom before the awesome face of the sovereign Lord...."[1]

God wants us to trust Him enough to cry out to Him with our laments. Expressing our complaints and grief to the Lord unburdens our souls and enables us to be more receptive to God's counsel. At the same time, we also need to trust what Scripture says, that one day God will execute justice in the world.

For the Lord will not forsake
his people; he will not abandon
his heritage; for justice will
return to the righteous....
PSALM 94:14–16

The Bible tells us that at His return, Christ will deal justly with sin and evil.[2] All things in our present world that are so wrong will be done away with. Jesus will "take away" the sin of the world for every believer.[3]

Affirm God's Offer

If you or a loved one is near death, a major concern may be, "Do I need to fear the judgment of God?" The word judgment has negative overtones, and it can strike fear in our hearts.

For we must all appear before the judgment seat of Christ, so that each one may receive what is due for what he has done in the body, whether good or evil.

2 CORINTHIANS 5:10

After reading this verse, we might think we should add up our good deeds to see how they compare with any bad deeds. But if the bad outweighs the good, then what? What is the standard by which we are saved from God's wrath against sin? Jesus said, *"Be perfect as your heavenly Father is perfect"* (MATTHEW 5:48). How can we possibly measure up, especially when we remember all of our past sins?

The only way we can meet this standard is if God Himself gives us a share in Christ's own righteousness. What good works must we do to earn this gift of His righteousness? None. It is freely given to us by Christ.

The righteousness of Christ enters our lives when we receive it by faith in Christ.

The righteous shall live by faith.
ROMANS 1:17

If God were to ask you, "Why should I let you into heaven?" you can answer, "I believe in Jesus Christ, and I receive His righteousness to cover my sin."

For all have sinned and fall short
of the glory of God, and all are
justified freely by his grace through

*the redemption that came by
Christ Jesus. God presented Christ
as a sacrifice of atonement,
through the shedding of his
blood—to be received by faith.*
ROMANS 3:23–25 NIV

This is *astonishingly good news!*
Righteousness—being right with God—
is a gift God gives to whoever believes
in Jesus Christ. To be righteous does
not depend on how many good deeds
we have done. Rather, to be righteous
depends on Christ's righteousness, trans-
ferred to us by grace when we believe
in Christ. Thus, salvation is a gift of
God's grace, His unmerited favor.

*By grace you have been saved
through faith. And this is not your
own doing; it is the gift of God,
not a result of works....*
EPHESIANS 2:8–9

Are "works" of any value? Yes, they are the outward demonstration of inner faith. We can and should live out our faith with good works, motivated by gratitude—gratitude for God's generosity and love working in us by His grace.

Does a believer in Jesus Christ need to fear God's judgment? No! At the final judgment, God will judge those who believe in Christ to have received the righteousness of Christ. As a follower of Jesus, you will be justified before God—just as if you had never sinned!

There is therefore now no condemnation for those who are in Christ Jesus.... What then shall we say to these things? If God is for us, who can be against us?

ROMANS 8:1, 31

What about those who reject the grace of God and refuse to trust in

Jesus for rescue from the wrath of God against sin? Scripture suggests that God will allow them to experience the consequences of their choice—as awful as that may be.[4] None of us is in a position to condemn anyone else, because only God knows the true heart of a person.[5]

Jesus invites you to open the door of your heart to Him.[6] If you have not yet committed yourself to Christ in faith, you can pray now: "God, I'm sorry for my sins. Please forgive me. I trust Jesus to be my Savior and Lord."

For God so loved the world,
that he gave his only Son,
that whoever believes in him
should not perish but have eternal
life. For God did not send his
Son into the world to condemn
the world, but in order that the
world might be saved through
him. Whoever believes in him
is not condemned, but whoever

does not believe is condemned
already, because he has not believed
in the name of the only Son of God.
JOHN 3:16–18

Think of it: God loves you! Let us receive God's good news as the ground receives rain, and be astonished that He showers us with His amazing grace!

My wife, Janiece, experienced a poignant deathbed moment with her mother. When Janiece said to her, "If God were to ask you, 'Why should I let you into heaven?' what would you say?" After a long silence, her mother answered, "Only Jesus." It is a precious memory of her mother's faith in Christ. Can you testify, as well, to your faith in Jesus?

I know not why God's
wondrous grace to me
he has made known,
nor why, unworthy,
Christ in love redeemed

me for his own. But I
know whom I have believed,
and am persuaded
that he is able to keep
that which I've committed
unto him against that day.[7]

****

Summary

When we appear before God on the day of judgment, the ultimate question to be answered is, "Why would God forgive you?" On the basis of Scripture, you can answer, "Only Jesus." Jesus has paid all the penalty for our sin. He thereby acquits, frees, and releases us from the judgment our sin deserves and gives us eternal life.

Prayer

Dear Jesus Christ, You are Lord of the universe. You are our coming Judge and Redeemer. I humbly repent of my sin and receive You as my Savior and Lord. Thank You for dying on the cross to pay the penalty I deserve to pay for my sin. Thank You for offering me complete forgiveness now and solid hope for eternity. Amen.

Affirmation

Question: "What is your only comfort, in life and in death?"

Answer: "That I belong—body and soul, in life and in death—not to myself but to my faithful Savior, Jesus Christ, who at the cost of his own blood has fully paid for all my sins and has completely freed me from the dominion of the devil; that he protects me so well that without the will of my Father in heaven not a hair can fall from my head; indeed, that everything must fit his purpose for my salvation. Therefore, by his Holy Spirit, he also assures me of eternal life...."[8]

Reflection

1. When you think about the "judgment of God," what comes to your mind?
2. If you wrote a lament, what anguish would you communicate to God?
3. Why is God's judgment good news for the believer?

*I [Jesus] am with you always,
to the end of the age.*

MATTHEW 28:20

CHAPTER 6

What Is the Meaning of the "New Heavens and New Earth"?

According to his promise we are waiting for new heavens and a new earth in which righteousness dwells.

2 PETER 3:13

Many people are confused as to what the Bible teaches about the new heavens and the new earth. Some commentators have contributed to the confusion by adding wild imagination to what the Scripture says. Perhaps at the return of Christ, which inaugurates the new heavens and new earth, everyone will be surprised.

Although details of our eternal existence are a mystery, the Bible does give us a few remarkable descriptions of the promised new creation. Here are three.

1. The earth will be made new.

Can you imagine what the Garden of Eden was like in all of its pristine grandeur? Think of the most beautiful places you have ever visited. The new earth is expected to be like those beautiful places, only better. The curse brought into the world by sin will be reversed.

In 2 PETER 3:13, quoted at the beginning of this chapter, Peter teaches that the heavens and earth will be new. He echoes the prophet Isaiah, who also foretold God's promise:

> *For behold, I create new*
> *heavens and a new earth....*
> ISAIAH 65:17

Do the words *new earth* mean an earth totally different from the earth we know now, or do they mean a restoration of our current earth? The Greek word for "new" suggests *restoration*.[1] Peter reminds his readers:

> *God [will] restore everything,*
> *as he promised long ago through*
> *his holy prophets.*
> ACTS 3:21 NIV

Restoration suggests *continuity*—connection with the old, the familiar, the well-known, but also a *discontinuity*—forming something new. We could compare this to having a child. When a child is born, the child is, of course, human, like the parents. But the child is also fresh, unique—not the same individual as the parents. The new earth will be like that—familiar, yet wonderfully new.

What will life on this new earth be like? Ponder this magnificent description found in Revelation 21:

> *Then I saw "a new heaven and a new earth," for the first heaven and the first earth had passed away, and there was no longer any sea. I saw the Holy City, the new Jerusalem, coming down out of heaven from God, prepared as a bride beautifully dressed for her husband. And I heard a loud voice from the throne saying, "Look! God's dwelling place is now among the people, and he will dwell with them. They will be his people,*

*and God himself will be with them
and be their God. 'He will wipe
every tear from their eyes. There will
be no more death' or mourning or
crying or pain, for the old order of
things has passed away."*
REVELATION 21:1–4 NIV

Imagine these glorious qualities listed in Revelation 21:

- A new heaven and a new earth
- No sea (a symbol of evil)
- The holy city (the people of God)
- God Himself will dwell with us
- No more tears
- No more death
- No more mourning or crying or pain!

Wow!

2. Heaven and the earth will be one.

Heaven is God's "space." In REVELATION 21:1–3, we learn that God will make the new earth His dwelling place. Because heaven is where God is, we shall then be in heaven while we are on the new earth.

Bible scholar Anthony Hoekema explains: "Heaven and earth will then no longer be separated, as they are now, but will be one."[2]

What about the popular notion of heaven being somewhere up in space, where we wear white robes and play harps? That's not what the Scripture teaches. But there will be music and song there, because they so powerfully express our deepest emotions. We will employ music in the praise of Christ.[3]

Praise, my soul, the King of heaven;
to his feet your tribute bring,
ransomed, healed, restored, forgiven,

evermore his praises sing.
Alleluia, alleluia!
Praise the everlasting King![4]

Praise gives voice to our souls. "The Bible assures us," says Hoekema, "that God will create a new earth on which we shall live to God's praise in glorified, resurrected bodies. On that new earth, therefore, we hope to spend eternity, enjoying its beauties, exploring its resources, and using its treasures to the glory of God."[5]

3. Righteousness will permeate the new heavens and the new earth.

The apostle Peter wrote that God has promised us new heavens and a new earth *where righteousness dwells.*[6] That means that every believer will be free from sin, free from a me-centered pride, free from prejudice, hate, and injustice.

"Righteousness" does not pervade this earth now, but on the new earth there will be no need for police or an army. You will not need to lock your home. You will not worry about corruption or serial killers or terrorism.

Righteousness will dwell on the new earth because God dwells there. God's righteousness is just and true. It will permeate every relationship with fullness and completeness. We will not feel alone or misunderstood. We will have perfect communication. Every activity will be inspired by whatever is excellent and commendable. Finally, the petition in the Lord's Prayer will be fully realized:

Your kingdom come, your will
be done, on earth as it is in heaven.
MATTHEW 6:10

Prepare to be surprised by the new heavens and new earth. Remember what the apostle Paul reminded the Corinthian Christians:

No eye has seen, nor ear heard,
nor the heart of man imagined,
what God has prepared for those
who love him.

1 CORINTHIANS 2:9

****

Summary

At the return of Christ, heaven and earth will be one, the earth will be newly restored, and righteousness will permeate the new heavens and earth. God will grant us a joy and a peace beyond what this current earth can offer. The wonder of it all helps us now to look forward to the coming glory.

Prayer/Poem

O God of wonder,
God of might,
Grant us some elevated sight,
Of endless days.
And let us see
The joy of what is yet to be....

The blind can see
a bird on wing,
The dumb can lift
their voice and sing.
The diabetic eats at will,
The coronary runs uphill.
The lame can walk,
the deaf can hear,
The cancer-ridden bone
is clear.
Arthritic joints are lithe
and free, And every
pain has ceased to be.
And every sorrow deep within

And every trace of
lingering sin is gone.
And all that's left is joy,
And endless ages to employ
The heart and mind,
and understand and love
the sovereign Lord
who planned that it should take
eternity to lavish all
his grace on me....

And guard us by the hope
that we, through grace
on lands you restore,
are justified for evermore.[7]
(A prayer by John Piper)

Reflection

1. What is the most beautiful place you have ever seen? How would you describe it?
2. What excites you the most about the new heavens and the new earth?
3. What comforts you the most in this chapter?

Praise to the Lord,
the Almighty, the King of creation!
O my soul, praise him,
for he is your health and salvation![8]

Praise the Lord, my soul;
all my inmost being,
praise his holy name.
Praise the Lord, my soul,
and forget not all his benefits—
who forgives all your sins and
heals all your diseases,
who redeems your life from the pit
and crowns you with love
and compassion.

PSALM 103:1–4 NIV

CHAPTER 7

What Comfort Do I Have Now?

And when the chief Shepherd appears,
you will receive the unfading
crown of glory.

1 PETER 5:4

P eter wrote that when Jesus appears at His return, you will receive a crown of glory that will never fade. It will be eternal glory.

You or a loved one might be in a debilitating condition right now. Pain and sadness hang heavy over you like a dark cloud, and it's difficult for you to see any light, any hope. If I were sitting with you, I would listen to your story. Each condition is different; each presents its own challenges. When we had explored adequately how you think and feel, I would gently suggest we turn to Scripture and hear what our Wonderful Counselor would offer as comfort.

The Promised Winner's Crown

I think Jesus would comfort us by saying that your reward is coming. Paul anticipated the winner's crown.

Now there is in store for me the crown of righteousness, which the Lord, the righteous Judge, will award to me on that day—and not only to me, but also to all who have longed for his appearing.

2 TIMOTHY 4:8

Again, Paul used a sports analogy. "Crown" relates to the Olympic wreath given in ancient times to champions who had endured obstacles and won the contest. The crown consisted of flowers that did not last. Like any achievement in this life, the exhilaration we can get from those wins is limited. But Scripture reminds us that the victor's crown that Jesus gives to every believer is not temporary; it will not fade.

When Paul mentioned the "crown of righteousness," he was referring to the marvelous, redeeming righteousness that our Lord Jesus Christ will confer on every believer. If this crown was the result of our own efforts, its value would be temporary. But, in fact, this crown was won by Christ's death and resurrection. It's good eternally. As we look forward in hope to this "unfading crown of glory," as Peter calls it, we can experience comfort even now as we anticipate the victory.

The Glory of God

I think Jesus would comfort us by directing our attention to God's glory. As Paul suggested to the Roman Christians, God's glory is inexhaustible. It will take "forever" to explore. We will be eternally grateful for the riches of His grace toward us and His glory in us.

Have you ever wondered what the "glory of God" means? In one sense, it includes all God has done in the history of our redemption. Its significance is substantial or heavy. Paul talks about the "weight of glory":

So we do not lose heart. Though our outer self is wasting away, our inner self is being renewed day by day. For this light momentary affliction is preparing for us an eternal weight of glory beyond all comparison.

2 CORINTHIANS 4:16–17

Wendell Kimbrough put this sense of glory to music:

> *Oh eternal weight of glory,*
> *Oh inheritance divine, we will*
> *see our Lord redeeming*
> *every past and future time.*
> *All our pains will be transfigured*
> *like the scars of Christ our Lord,*
> *we will see the weight of glory*
> *and our broken years restored.*
> *For behold I tell a mystery:*
> *at the trumpet sound we'll wake!*
> *Every year we thought was wasted,*
> *every night we cried, "How Long?"*
> *All will be a passing moment*
> *in our Savior's victory song.*[1]

Glory refers to God being "loaded" with infinite holiness, expressed in His grace, power, beauty, goodness, justice, and love. When we glorify God, we honor Him for all that He is. Each quality is displayed with dazzling brilliance in Jesus Christ.

> *Long ago, at many times and in many ways, God spoke to our fathers by the prophets, but in these last days he has spoken to us by his Son, whom he appointed the heir of all things, through whom also he created the world. [The Son] is the radiance of the glory of God.*
>
> HEBREWS 1:1–3

The radiance of Jesus is reflected in the creation of the world and in the new creation within every believer!

> *God has chosen to make known...the glorious riches of this mystery, which is Christ in you, the hope of glory.*
>
> COLOSSIANS 1:27 NIV

The "hope of glory" is not wishful thought, but a confident, jubilant knowledge in the present that one day we will see Christ face to face.

For now we see in a mirror dimly, but then face to face. Now I know in part; then I shall know fully, even as I have been fully known.
1 CORINTHIANS 13:12

I find this enormously exciting.

The Power of Prayer

I think Jesus would comfort us by calling us to prayer. Before Jesus' death, the Bible says that He was sorrowful and troubled. For strength, for comfort, for courage, He prayed to God the Father, asking that He would not have to face the ordeal of the *cup*— bearing the sins of the whole world in

His death on the cross. Yet He wanted to follow the Father's plan for Him.

My Father, if it be possible, let this cup pass from me; nevertheless, not as I will, but as you will.
MATTHEW 26:39

When we feel weak, and when the path before us seems impassable, let us remember that we are not alone in our effort to communicate with God:

The Spirit helps us in our weakness. For we do not know what to pray for as we ought, but the Spirit himself intercedes for us with groanings too deep for words.
ROMANS 8:26

Is there someone whom you can ask to pray for you? Jesus asked His disciples to pray with Him. JAMES 5:16 calls us to *"pray for one another."* Praying together with family and friends enables us to experience powerful support as brothers and sisters in Christ.

What is prayer? Certainly, it includes asking for things—healing, relief from suffering, a change of heart—but it also includes praise, confession, and communion with God. Prayer establishes a connection with the One who knows all about our troubles; who knows our past, present, and future perfectly; who has "the whole world in His hands." Prayer is talking—and listening—with a Friend who loves us with an everlasting love.

In my own experience, prayer has been a means of comforting my troubled soul. Remembering that God loves me and is in control frees me from worry. It encourages me to unburden my anxious fears to our Wonderful Counselor and to continue on the journey ahead of me, refreshed. It enables me to pray with Christ, "not my will, but Your will be done."

The Encouragement of Scripture

I think Jesus, our Wonderful Counselor, would comfort us now by reminding us of His Word to us. His Word comforts me. As my physical condition worsens, I am tempted to despair. Then I remember what some famous theologian said: "Sometimes you need to beat yourself over the head with Scripture." For this hardheaded Dutchman, I think that is exactly right.

So, I search for Scripture passages that remind me of God's good news. I read them over and memorize some of them. Listed below are some verses that renew my mind. As you reflect on them, you, too, will find your mind *renewed*, and as the apostle Paul says, you will be *transformed*.[2] You may want to get your mind refreshed now as a helpful preparation for the coming glory celebration.

The LORD is my strength and my song, and he has become my salvation; He is my God, and I will praise him.
EXODUS 15:2

Be strong and courageous. Do not fear... for it is the Lord your God who goes with you. He will not leave you or forsake you.
DEUTERONOMY 31:6

I bless the Lord who gives me counsel; in the night also my heart instructs me. I have set the Lord always before me; because he is at my right hand, I shall not be shaken.
PSALM 16:7–8

I love you, O Lord, my strength. The Lord is my rock and my fortress and my deliverer, my God, my rock, in whom I take refuge, my shield, and the horn of my salvation, my stronghold. I call upon the Lord, who is worthy to be praised.

PSALM 18:1–3

The Lord is my shepherd; I shall not want.... Even though I walk through the valley of the shadow of death, I will fear no evil, for you are with me.... Surely goodness and mercy shall follow me all the days of my life, and I shall dwell in the house of the Lord forever.

PSALM 23:1, 4, 6

I trust in you, O Lord; I say, "You are my God." My times are in your hand.

PSALM 31:14–15

Precious in the sight of the Lord is the death of his saints.

PSALM 116:15

Peace I [Jesus] leave with you; my peace I give to you. Not as the world gives do I give to you. Let not your hearts be

troubled, neither let them be afraid.
JOHN 14:27

I am sure that neither death nor life...
nor things present nor things to come...
nor anything else in all creation, will be
able to separate us from the love of God
in Christ Jesus our Lord.
ROMANS 8:38–39

I am continually with you; you hold my
right hand. You guide me with your
counsel, and afterward you will receive
me to glory.
PSALM 73:23–24

The time of my departure has come.
I have fought the good fight, I have
finished the race, I have kept the faith.
Henceforth there is laid up for me the
crown of righteousness, which the Lord,
the righteous judge, will award to me
on that day.
2 TIMOTHY 4:6–8

Behold! I tell you a mystery. We shall not all sleep, but we shall all be changed, in a moment, in the twinkling of an eye, at the last trumpet. For the trumpet will sound, and the dead will be raised imperishable, and we shall be changed.... Then shall come to pass the saying that is written: "Death is swallowed up in victory.""O death, where is your victory? O death, where is your sting?" The sting of death is sin, and the power of sin is the law. But thanks be to God, who gives us the victory through our Lord Jesus Christ.

1 CORINTHIANS 15:51–52, 54–57

Oh, the depth of the riches and wisdom and knowledge of God! How unsearchable are his judgments and how inscrutable his ways! For from him and through him and to him are all things. To [God] be glory forever. Amen.

ROMANS 11:33, 36

****

Summary

Dear friends, when the last trumpet sounds and the great resurrection bell resounds, "paradise lost" will become "paradise found," and you and I will celebrate the glory of God. We are comforted now by the confident hope of beholding God's glory. Praise the Lord!

Prayer/Doxology

Praise God from whom all blessings flow;
Praise him, all creatures here below;
Praise him above, ye heavenly host
Praise Father, Son, and Holy Ghost.
Amen.[3]

Reflection

1. What feelings do you think you will have when you finally receive the "winner's crown"?
2. What do you imagine will be your response when you see the glory of God?
3. Who are two or three people you can ask to pray with you?
4. As you review the Scriptures listed in this chapter, what passage is most helpful to you right now?
5. On what comfort in this chapter will you choose to focus?

Blessed be the God and Father of our Lord Jesus Christ! According to his great mercy, he has caused us to be born again to a living hope through the resurrection of Jesus Christ from the dead, to an inheritance that is imperishable, undefiled, and unfading, kept in heaven for you....

And after you have suffered a little while, the God of all grace, who has called you to his eternal glory in Christ, will himself restore, confirm, strengthen, and establish you.

1 PETER 1:3–4; 5:10

Notes

A Note to the Reader

1. J. Todd Billings, *Rejoicing in Lament: Wrestling with Incurable Cancer and Life in Christ* (Brazos Press, 2015), 33.

Chapter 1: How Can I Prepare for My Departure?

1. "The Strife Is O'er, the Battle Done," *Lift Up Your Hearts: Psalms, Hymns, and Spiritual Songs* (Faith Alive, 2013), 185.
2. "For All the Saints," *Lift Up Your Hearts: Psalms, Hymns, and Spiritual Songs* (Faith Alive, 2013), 254.

Chapter 2: What Happens Right after Death?

1. N.T. Wright, *Surprised by Hope: Rethinking Heaven, the Resurrection, and the Mission of the Church* (Harper One, 2008), 171–172.

2. "Going Home," words by William Arms Fisher and Ken Bible, music by Antonin Dvorak; arranged by Ken Bible, 2000, by LNWhymns.com. CCLI Song #3636552. (A video depicting images related to the music and lyrics can be seen on YouTube at "Annie Haslam—Going Home").

3. "Precious Lord, Take My Hand," Thomas A. Dorsey, *Lift Up Your Hearts: Psalms, Hymns, and Spiritual Songs* (Faith Alive, 2013), 465; text copyright © 1938, 1966 (ren.) Warner-Tamerlane Publishing Corp. Tune copyright adapt. © 1938, 1966, (ren.) Warner-Tamerlane Publishing

Chapter 3: How Can I Get Ready for the Return of Christ?

1. ROMANS 8:11: *And if the Spirit of him who raised Jesus from the dead is living in you, he who raised Christ from the dead will also give life to your mortal bodies because of his Spirit who lives in you.*

2. MATTHEW 24:14: *And this gospel of the kingdom will be proclaimed throughout the whole world as a testimony to all nations, and then the end will come.*

3. PHILIPPIANS 2:9–11: *Therefore God has highly exalted him and bestowed on him the name that is above every name, so that at the name of Jesus every knee should bow, in heaven and on earth and under the earth, and every tongue confess that Jesus Christ is Lord, to the glory of God the Father.*

4. MATTHEW 25:31–46: *When the Son of Man comes in his glory, and all the angels with him, then he will sit on his glorious throne. Before him will be gathered all the nations, and he will separate people one from another as a shepherd separates the sheep from the goats. And he will place the sheep on his right, but the goats on the left. Then the King will say to those on his right, "Come, you who are blessed by my Father, inherit the kingdom prepared for you from the foundation of the world. For I was hungry and you gave me food, I was thirsty and you gave me drink, I was a stranger and you welcomed me, I was naked and you clothed me, I was sick and you visited me, I was in prison and you came to me." Then the righteous will answer him, saying, "Lord, when did we see you hungry and feed you, or thirsty and give you drink? And when did we see you a stranger and welcome you, or naked and clothe you? And when did we see* *you sick or in prison and visit you?" And the King will answer them, "Truly, I say to you, as you did it to one of the least of these my brothers, you did it to me." Then he will say to those on his left, "Depart from me, you cursed, into the eternal fire prepared for the devil and his angels. For I was hungry and you gave me no food, I was thirsty and you gave me no drink, I was a stranger and you did not welcome me, naked and you did not clothe me, sick and in prison and you did not visit me." Then they also will answer, saying, "Lord, when did we see you hungry or thirsty or a stranger or naked or sick or in prison, and did not minister to you? Then he will answer them, saying, "Truly, I say to you, as you did not do it to one of the least of these, you did not do it to me." And these will go away into eternal punishment, but the righteous into eternal life.*

5. ROMANS 2:5: *But because of your hard and impenitent heart you are storing up*

wrath for yourself on the day of wrath when God's righteous judgment will be revealed.

6. MATTHEW 25:34: *Then the King will say..."Come, you who are blessed by my Father, inherit the kingdom prepared for you from the foundation of the world."*

7. 2 PETER 3:13: *But according to his promise we are waiting for new heavens and a new earth in which righteousness dwells.*

8. The big bang theory is a leading scientific explanation about how the universe began. GENESIS 1:1 says, *In the beginning, God created the heavens and the earth.*

9. Some scientists, such as Professor Brian Cox, predict the end of the universe. In his Wonders of the Solar System and Wonders of the Universe series, he predicts that everything, including time itself, will cease to exist. MATTHEW 24:14 states, *And this gospel of the kingdom will be proclaimed*

throughout the whole world as a testimony to all nations, and then the end will come.

10. There are differing views about the sequence of events at the return of Christ. While respecting other biblical interpretations, I take the position that the events related to the return of Christ will occur rather simultaneously.

11. MATTHEW 25:1–13: *The Parable of the Ten Virgins: Then the kingdom of heaven will be like ten virgins who took their lamps and went to meet the bridegroom. Five of them were foolish, and five were wise. For when the foolish took their lamps, they took no oil with them, but the wise took flasks of oil with their lamps. As the bridegroom was delayed, they all became drowsy and slept. But at midnight there was a cry, "Here is the bridegroom! Come out to meet him." Then all those virgins rose and trimmed their lamps. And the foolish said to the*

wise, "Give us some of your oil, for our lamps are going out." But the wise answered, saying, "Since there will not be enough for us and for you, go rather to the dealers and buy for yourselves." And while they were going to buy, the bridegroom came, and those who were ready went in with him to the marriage feast, and the door was shut. Afterward the other virgins came also, saying, "Lord, lord, open to us." But he answered, "Truly, I say to you, I do not know you." Watch therefore, for you know neither the day nor the hour.

12. A part of liturgy expressed by many Christians. Most English versions of the Nicene Creed also include the following statements: "...he ascended into heaven and is seated at the right hand of the Father. He will come again in his glory to judge the living and the dead, and his kingdom will have no end.... We look for the

resurrection of the dead, and the life of the world to come."

13. "My Hope Is Built on Nothing Less," Edward Mote, *Lift Up Your Hearts: Psalms, Hymns, and Spiritual Songs* (Faith Alive, 2013), 772.

14. "Eternal Weight of Glory," Wendell Kimbrough, from the album *Psalms We Sing Together*, 2016. wendellk.com.

Chapter 4: What Will Our Bodily Resurrection Be Like?

1. See REVELATION 21:3–4: *And I heard a loud voice from the throne saying, "Behold, the dwelling place of God is with man. He will dwell with them, and they will be his people, and God himself will be with them as their God. He will wipe away every tear from their eyes, and death shall be no more, neither shall there be mourning, nor crying, nor pain anymore, for the former things have*

passed away." Also see Anthony A. Hoekema, The Bible and the Future (William B. Eerdmans, 1979), 249.

2. Hoekema, 249.

3. Hoekema, 250.

Chapter 5: How Can I Face God's Judgment?

1. J. Todd Billings, *Rejoicing in Lament: Wrestling with Incurable Cancer and Life in Christ* (Brazos Press, 2015), 22.

2. ACTS 17:31: *For he has set a day when he will judge the world with justice by the man he has appointed. He has given proof of this to everyone by raising him from the dead* (NIV).

3. JOHN 1:29: *The next day he saw Jesus coming toward him, and said, "Behold, the Lamb of God, who takes away the sin of the world!"*

4. JOHN 3:18: *Whoever believes in him is not condemned, but whoever does not believe is condemned already, because he*

has not believed in the name of the only Son of God.

ROMANS 1:18–32: *For the wrath of God is revealed from heaven against all ungodliness and unrighteousness of men, who by their unrighteousness suppress the truth. For what can be known about God is plain to them, because God has shown it to them. For his invisible attributes, namely, his eternal power and divine nature, have been clearly perceived, ever since the creation of the world, in the things that have been made. So they are without excuse. For although they knew God, they did not honor him as God or give thanks to him, but they became futile in their thinking, and their foolish hearts were darkened. Claiming to be wise, they became fools, and exchanged the glory of the immortal God for images resembling mortal man and birds and animals and creeping things. Therefore God gave them up in the lusts of their hearts to impurity, to the dishonoring of their bodies among themselves, because they exchanged the truth about God for a lie and worshiped and served the creature rather than the Creator, who is blessed forever! Amen. For this reason God gave them up to dishonorable passions. For their women exchanged natural relations for those that are contrary to nature; and the men likewise gave up natural relations with women and were consumed with passion for one another, men committing shameless acts with men and receiving in themselves the due penalty for their error. And since they did not see fit to acknowledge God, God gave them up to a debased mind to do what ought not to be done. They were filled with all manner of unrighteousness, evil, covetousness, malice. They are full of envy, murder, strife, deceit, maliciousness. They are gossips, slanderers, haters of God, insolent, haughty, boastful, inventors of evil, disobedient to parents, foolish, faithless, heartless, ruthless. Though they know God's righteous decree that those who practice such things deserve to die, they not only do them but give approval to those who practice them.*

5. ROMANS 2:1–4: *Therefore you have no excuse, O man, every one of you who judges. For in passing judgment on another you condemn yourself, because you, the judge, practice the very same things. We know that the judgment of God rightly falls on those who practice such things. Do you suppose, O man— you who judge those who practice such things and yet do them yourself—that you will escape the judgment of God? Or do you presume on the riches of his kindness and forbearance and patience, not knowing that God's kindness is meant to lead you to repentance?*

6. REVELATION 3:20: *Behold, I stand at the door and knock. If anyone hears my voice and opens the door, I will come in to him and eat with him, and he with me.*

7. "I Know Not Why God's Wondrous Grace," Daniel W. Whittle, *Lift Up Your Hearts: Psalms, Hymns, and Spiritual Songs* (Faith Alive, 2013), 690.

8. *The Heidelberg Catechism* (United Church Press, 1962), 9.

Chapter 6: What Is the Meaning of the "New Heavens and New Earth"?

1. The Greek word for "new" in 2 PETER 3:13 is *kainos*, not *neos*. *Kainos* means "new in nature or quality," not "new in origin." The newness in creation is therefore refined or restored and has continuity with the present cosmos.

2. Anthony A. Hoekema, *The Bible and the Future* (William B. Eerdmans, 1979), 274.

3. See, for example, REVELATION 5:9–10.

4. "Praise, My Soul, the King of Heaven" Henry F. Lyte, *Lift Up Your*

Hearts: Psalms, Hymns, and Spiritual Songs (Faith Alive, 2013), 571.

5. Hoekema, 274, REVELATION 5:10.

6. 2 PETER 3:13: *But according to his promise we are waiting for new heavens and a new earth in which righteousness dwells.*

7. "Justified For Evermore," from *Future Grace, Revised Edition: The Purifying Power of the Promises of God* by John Piper, copyright © 1995, 2012 by Desiring God Foundation. WaterBrook-Multnomah is an imprint of the Crown Publishing Group, a division of Penguin Random House LLC. All rights reserved.

8. "Praise to the Lord, the Almighty," Lift Up Your Hearts: Psalms, Hymns, and Spiritual Songs (Faith Alive,2013), 575.

Chapter 7: What Comfort Do I Have Now?

1. "Eternal Weight of Glory," words and music by Wendell Kimbrough, 2016. From the album *Psalms We Sing Together*. wendellk.com.

2. ROMANS 12:2: *Do not be conformed to this world, but be transformed by the renewal of your mind.*

3. "Praise God from Whom All Blessings Flow," *Lift Up Your Hearts: Psalms, Hymns, and Spiritual Songs* (Faith Alive,2013), 965.

Acknowledgments

1. "To God Be the Glory," Fanny J. Crosby *Lift Up Your Hearts: Psalms, Hymns, and Spiritual Songs* (Faith Alive, 2013), 604.

Summaries

Chapter 1: How Can I Prepare for My Departure?

You can prepare for your departure by affirming your belief in Jesus Christ, who loves you and gives you eternal life.

Chapter 2: What Happens Right after Death?

Right after death, the soul of the believer is "at home with the Lord," and that is better than we can imagine.

Chapter 3: How Can I Get Ready for the Return of Christ?

When we set our hope on Jesus, who is our strength and who comforts us in our weakness, we will be ready for His return.

Chapter 4: What Will Our Bodily Resurrection Be Like?

The Bible's description of our resurrected bodies is that they will be imperishable, glorious, powerful, spiritual bodies. This gives us hope now, knowing that God will give us the final victory over every consequence of sin.

Chapter 5: How Can I Face God's Judgment?

When we appear before God on the day of judgment, the ultimate question to be answered is, "Why would God forgive you?" On the basis of Scripture, you can answer, "Only Jesus." Jesus has paid all the penalty for our sin. He thereby acquits, frees, and releases us from the judgment our sin deserves and gives us eternal life.

Chapter 6: What Is the Meaning of the "New Heavens and New Earth"?

At the return of Christ, heaven and earth will be one, the earth will be newly restored, and righteousness will permeate the new heavens and earth. God will grant us a joy and a peace beyond what this present world can offer. The wonder of it all helps us now to look forward to the coming glory.

Chapter 7: What Comfort Do I Have Now?

Dear friends, when the last trumpet sounds and the great resurrection bell resounds, "paradise lost" will become "paradise found," and you and I will celebrate the glory of God. We are comforted now by the confident hope of beholding God's glory. Praise the Lord!

Let us hold unswervingly to the hope we profess, for he who promised is faithful.

HEBREWS 10:23 NIV

A Lament

by

Don Sinnema

It was graduation day at Trinity Christian College when I took Lois to the emergency room, where she was diagnosed with bile duct cancer. The doctors gave her three months to a year to live; the Lord gave us twenty-five months.

We prayed fervently for healing; you prayed for healing, and many others—even people we do not know personally—prayed for her healing.

But healing did not come. Three months ago, the medical establishment gave up, and Lois entered hospice care at home. For weeks she clung to life, but a week ago Monday she began to decline quickly, and by Thursday morning the cancer had sapped every drop of life from her frail body. The Lord graciously took her gently into His arms.

I am most grateful to all of you for coming this evening to join our family as we remember Lois's life, and lament her death. Thank you for sitting down beside us on our mourning bench.

I did not look forward to Lois's death, nor did she. She and I could take comfort that she would soon be with the Lord, but never could we look forward to her death—not just the moment of death, but the dying.

I must now learn to live without her, but I cannot make peace with Lois' death. There is no peace in death.

Death is awful; death is abnormal, unnatural; death is the mortal enemy of life, not the natural end of a normal life. Indeed, death is demonic.

Cancer is demonic; it slowly eats away at life, and finally kills it.

So, I face Lois' death with indignation—not against God, though sometimes I wonder: *Why? Why?*

Rather, my indignation is against the powers of darkness, against Satan, against the evil that causes death.

Our God is a God of life, a God of health, well-being, *shalom*. God created us and meant for us to *live*—and thrive in the land of the living.

Death must really hurt Him. So, as we weep, I'm sure God's tears mingle with ours on this mourning bench.

I face Lois' death with indignation and grief because:

- Satan afflicted her with a long, slow death—for two difficult years with ongoing treatments, multiple complications, and unrelenting aches—until she was so depleted she could not even suck liquid up a straw.

- Death has ripped her from the prime of life, at age fifty-six, when she still had so much to contribute, so many songs to play, so many books to read, so much joy to give to our family and others.
- Death has robbed her sisters, Mary, Ruth, and Jane; her brother, Sylvan, and her in-laws, nieces, and nephews of a loving and vibrant sibling, aunt, and family member.
- Death has robbed her many friends of a gracious and caring companion.
- Death has robbed the libraries where she worked as a lover of books and a patron-friendly librarian.
- The prince of death has robbed the Church of a wonderful musician,

pianist, and organist. She had a feel for playing the soul of a song, the music that lies in the pause between the notes.

- Death has robbed me of the music of my life, my soul mate, my faithful companion, my lover.

- Death has wrenched from me the intimacy of marriage. Though there were tender moments, for months I could not even give her a good hug—it hurt her too much. The constant ache inside was so sensitive that touching her body anywhere was annoying, even a back rub. For months I could not even kiss her on the lips, for fear of spreading some germ that might shorten her life.

- Death has robbed our three children—Heather, Ethan, and Lawren—of a tender, loving mother. They are in their twenties—too young to lose their mother.

- Death has robbed little Anthony and our future grandkids of a doting grandmother they will never know and never remember.

So, I walk this dark valley with a heavy heart. I lament her death. It is a time of tears. But I lament her death with hope.

I look with hope to that day when the Lord will finally vanquish Satan and evil, that day when cancer will be obliterated, that day when pain and tears and death will be no more.

Lois's remains will be buried in the little country cemetery in Alberta where my great-grandparents, my grandparents, my parents, and other family members are buried. There she will lie at rest in the shadow of the Almighty, and day after day the breath of the Almighty, the southwest wind, will whistle its gentle tune through the prairie grass that grows above her grave until that wondrous day of her Savior's return.

I look with hope to that day when Lois will be raised to new life—with a perfect, vibrant body, no longer emaciated by cancer—that day when her long, lithe piano fingers, perfectly restored, will once again dance on the keyboard as she accompanies *all of you* in a jubilant dance of praise to our Maker in the New Earth.

(Read at the memorial service for Lois Sinnema, held in Evergreen Park, Illinois, June 14, 2006)

Additional Resources

1. **Jon Brown**, "Recognizing Jesus," a recording of the memorial service for Dr. Margaret Van Wylen. Go to: **www.thecomingglory.com/memorial.**

2. **J. Todd Billings**, *Rejoicing in Lament*, Brazos Press, 2015. Diagnosed with a rare form of incurable cancer at the age of thirty-nine, Christian theologian Todd Billings began grappling with the hard theological questions we face in the midst of crisis: *Why me? Why now? Where is God in all of this?* Billings moves beyond pat answers toward hope in God's promises.

3. **Timothy Keller**, *The Reason for God*, Dutton, 2008. Dr. Keller responds to seven common objections to

Christianity raised by those searching for true faith.

4. **C.S. Lewis**, *Mere Christianity*, Harper Collins, 1980. This book has helped me and a multitude of people better understand the basics of the Christian faith minus the cultural embellishments we tend to add to the faith.

5. **Joni Eareckson Tada**, *When God Weeps*, Zondervan, 1997. Joni's thirty years spent in a wheelchair has given her a special understanding of God's connection with suffering and provides a great source of comfort.

6. **Granger Westburg**, *Good Grief*, Fortress Press, 1971, 2011. For fifty years, this classic text has helped millions of readers find comfort and rediscover hope after loss. *Good Grief* identifies ten stages of grief—shock, emotion, depression, physical distress, panic, guilt, anger, resistance, hope, and finally acceptance.

7. **Lee Strobel**, *The Case for Christianity*, Zondervan, 2014. Former-atheist-turned-Christian Lee Strobel uses his investigative journalistic skills to answer questions about the Bible, science, and history.

Acknowledgments

My earliest awareness of biblical teaching on life after death was from a sermon by my father, William A. Swets, on the topic, "The King Is Coming." I was about five years old, but I have never forgotten the impact it had on me.

During my early college years, I seriously questioned some of my foundational beliefs. How could such an astounding gospel be true? Through the study of God's Word, through living examples of gospel joy, and through reading *Mere Christianity* by C.S. Lewis, God roused me from intellectual slumber and spiritual lethargy.

Later at Hope College in Holland, Michigan, I had a professor who taught

Greek with a Hungarian accent and a delightful sense of humor. Dr. Joseph Ziros told some very sad stories about how the communists invaded the university where he taught and tortured him. One day he stopped his story and said to the class, "My dear Christian friends, you look like horses.... You have such long faces!... Let us live *sub specie aeternitatis*, under the viewpoint of eternity." This became basic to my world- and life-view.

Students, single adults, couples, and seniors, and colleagues at University Reformed Church in Ann Arbor, Michigan; Christ Community Church in Palm Springs, Florida; and Second Presbyterian Church in Memphis, Tennessee, all shaped and sharpened my ministry in pastoral care.

Dr. Suzanne McDonald, professor at Western Theological Seminary in Holland, Michigan, graciously allowed my wife and me to audit her course on eschatology, the biblical study of the fulfillment of all God's promises and purposes in the new creation. It provided us with a clearer "sneak preview" into the grand mystery of God's new creation plan.

Dr. Todd Billings, also a professor at Western Theological Seminary, helped me to reconsider the value of lament both in our discussions and through his excellent book, *Rejoicing in Lament*.

Dr. Gordon Van Wylen, Dr. James Bultman, Bob DeYoung, and Rev. Jonathon Brown formed a dream team of consultants and encouragers for this writing ministry.

Janiece S.S. Swets, who many years ago courageously agreed to partner with me as my wife, has daily offered me her love, wisdom, and ruthless editing competence...with humor and joy. I love her.

What incredible blessings from God these and so many others have been in my life. I'm profoundly grateful. To God be all glory!

To God Be the Glory

Great things he has taught us,
Great things he has done,
And great our rejoicing through
Jesus the Son;
But purer and higher and greater will be
Our wonder, our transport,
When Jesus we see.
Fanny J. Crosby[1]

About the Author

I learned caring ministry first from my father, William A. Swets, long before he served as the minister of pastoral care at Coral Ridge Presbyterian Church in Fort Lauderdale, Florida. Along with my mother, he parented me and my five sisters with gentle firmness and compassionate care.

At Hope College in Holland, Michigan, I majored in psychology because I wanted to know why people behave the way that they do. I wanted to know and positively influence others' behavior through the gifts, training, and circumstances I had been given.

During my junior year at Hope College, I asked myself how I could best use any gift granted to me. I came to believe that helping people to know God was the most important task for me, and I felt God was leading me to prepare for ministry at Western Theological Seminary in Holland, Michigan.

After serving as a campus minister at the University of Michigan, and the senior minister of a small church in Florida, I was called to be the minister of pastoral care at Second Presbyterian Church in Memphis, Tennessee.

The "time for my departure" is getting closer day by day. Although I deeply love this life, I can hardly wait for the coming glory.

Contact

I would love to hear from you. You may contact me at dr.swets@gmail.com. For further information, visit http://TheComingGlory.com.